SPEAKING OF GILL

SPEAKING OF GILL

Insights Into Public Speaking

James F. Gill

To order additional copies of this book, contact:
Xlibris Corporation
1-888-795-4274
www.Xlibris.com
Orders@Xlibris.com
33741

CONTENTS

FORWARD

In December 2002 I published my first book entitled *For James and Gillian*, dedicated to my grandchildren. I wanted them to know my history, what I believed in, how I conducted my life, and I wanted them to get it directly from me. It was a joy to write and it did much better than I had expected; so I decided to write another.

I have always been intrigued by the art of public speaking: the ability to convince an audience of the righteousness of a cause or the validity of a view point, to cause people to laugh or cry, to anger them, frighten them or inspire them, to stir them up or calm them down, to infuse them with pride, joy, regret or sorrow. I have done some public speaking and occasionally have offered suggestions to others such as former U.S. Senators Al D'Amato and Bob Dole, former New York Governor George Pataki, former New York City Mayor Rudy Giuliani, and former F.B.I. Director Louis J. Freeh.

Speaking in public is a fine art and a rare gift. Winston Churchill, the master, described it in these words: "Of all the talents bestowed upon men, none is so precious as the gift of oratory. He who enjoys it wields a power more durable than that of a king."

Many have used that gift to better mankind while others, such as Hitler, have misused it to inflict untolled and irreparable human misery. Oratorical ability is difficult to acquire but can be attained to a considerable degree, if certain fundamentals are applied. That is the subject matter of this book.

PART 1

Basic Principles

PART 1

Basic Principles

CHAPTER I

Be Not Afraid

Most people are frightened by the thought of addressing an audience. There is no need for such fear if you do your homework.

1) Know your audience. Take time out to learn about the organization you are addressing. What is its over-all mission; what are its interim goals; who are the leaders; who are the people in the audience; what do they favor; what do they oppose; who do they like; who do they dislike; what is the nature and purpose of the event?

   If you know your audience, you will avoid embarrassment and get an edge. If you don't, even the best have every reason to be fearful. Consider the experience of the late distinguished senator from New York, Daniel Patrick Moynihan, when he addressed the Friendly Sons of St. Patrick in 1977. It was a disaster because he hadn't assessed his audience beforehand.

   The Friendly Sons dinner is a black tie affair held on St. Patrick's Day. It is the largest dinner of the year, attended by approximately 3,000 men, mostly successful Irishmen. The Cardinal Archbishop of New York is the host and the speaker is introduced at about 9:30 p.m. at which time the audience expects to be entertained, not lectured.

At the outset, Moynihan referred to "Beyond The Melting Pot", a very serious treatise he had co-authored with Nathan Glazer, about the various ethnic groups of New York City, including of course, the Irish. After gratuitously criticizing The American Irish Historical Society (a sister organization to the Friendly Sons) and its members for lack of sophistication at one of his previous presentations—he plunged into a long, highly cerebral, incredibly convoluted and some times unintelligible diatribe, based in the main on the contents of "Beyond The Melting Pot."

The early resumption of conversations at tables throughout the room signaled that Moynihan had lost his audience. Instead of adapting to the situation, he plodded along and then began to berate his audience for not responding to him properly! This audacious blunder brought on cat-calls and heckling from people in the audience, which Moynihan began to answer from the podium. Finally he challenged one heckler to a fist fight! It was oratorical suicide, and Moynihan never attended another meeting of The Friendly Sons.

Before leaving Senator Moynihan, allow me to share with you a cardinal rule about public speaking. Never drink before you speak. While it may relax you a bit, it will dull your sensitivities at a time when you should be at your sharpest. Moreover, pre-speech anxiety is very common and indeed helpful because it gets the juices flowing.

2)   Continue to work on your speech until you are fully satisfied that it will be well received by your audience. That means re-drafting, making changes, additions and deletions. It means re-organizing, polishing, honing, shortening and adding punch.

3)   Check your speech to insure proper English grammar and usage. I may be more sensitive to English impropriety than others, but I find it disturbing and distracting. This is not the place for a course in proper English, but a few examples of very common errors may serve as reminders.

- You don't "*lay* down"
  you "*lie* down."
- You don't "*lie* the book on the table" you "*lay* the book on the table."
- "*Farther*" has to do with *distance*
  "*Further*" has to do with *degree*
- It's not "between you and *I*" it's "between you and *me*."
- If there are more than two persons present, it's not "*between* us," it's "*among* us."
- The verb "to be" never takes the objective case and therefore it's not "This is *him*," it's "This is *he*." It's not "Its *me*," it's "It is *I*."

I'll digress to share an Ed Koch story. The former Mayor is my friend and law partner and I march with him in the St. Patrick's Day Parade every year. Throughout the parade he thrusts his arms into the air and shouts out: "Its me". Ed is the most popular person in the parade and the crowd invariably responds with a roar. I once said to him: "Ed when, you say 'Its me', that is not grammatically correct. To be grammatically correct you should say: 'It is I.'" He looked at me with a gentle smile and said: "Jim, you're not really suggesting that I shout 'It is I' during the St. Patrick's Day Parade are you?'" and we laughed.

- Things don't center "*around*" something, they center "*on*" something.
- Churchill was once admonished for ending a sentence with a preposition. He denied having done so and added: "That is something up with which I would not put."

In any event, if you have any doubt, look it up. A good dictionary will usually provide the answer. Preferably, consult *Elements of Style* by William Stunk and E.B. White.

4)   After you have completed your speech, try it out on people knowledgeable about public speaking. Their reactions and suggestions are frequently of considerable value.

5)   Rehearse your timing and delivery until you are completely comfortable with it and it is second nature to you. When you deliver your speech, try not to read it word for word and look at your audience as much as possible. I also suggest that you memorize your opening and closing, so as to ensure audience eye contact during those important periods.

Some have great difficulty working off of a prepared text as opposed to speaking extemporaneously. Ed Koch, eschews prepared speeches and invariably speaks *ex tempore* from a few hand scribbled notes. Former Governor George Pataki prefers the same methodology, as did former Governors Nelson Rockefeller and Al Smith. While the spontaneity that approach generates can make for a more effective delivery—it is not recommended for the uninitiated.

Your finely tuned, well thought out, tried and tested prepared text, right there in front of you is your security blanket. Be sure that the print is sufficiently large, underscore the lines you want to emphasize, and insert "pause" lines where appropriate. Some even include written reminders as to gestures, as Churchill did. Put all of your trust and confidence into your *magnum opus* and let it fly! I always regard the delivery as the fun part and look forward to it. So should you.

Chapter II

Brevity is a Virtue

I have been to myriad dinners, luncheons and other events and suffered through hundreds of speeches. Most are dull, boring and much too long. You can sometimes get away with dull and boring, but you can never get away with too long. It is the most common failing of public speakers and it can be the most deadly. Thus, one of the fundamentals of public speaking: "You can never bomb short." Not grammatically correct—but to the point.

The late Owen McGivern, one of the finest after dinner speakers of our time, once told me that *no one* can hold the attention of an audience for more than 13 minutes!

Many public speakers get carried away endlessly with the over-riding importance of their sacred causes, or ramble on *ad nauseam* about the background of someone they are introducing, or seize the occasion to demonstrate how smart they are, or become enamored of their own speaking skills or mesmerized by the sound of their own voices, or in the worst possible case—all of the above. They become convinced that their audience is hanging on their every word—they are dead wrong. They are oblivious to certain basics concerning audiences: (1) most people have very short attention spans, (2) most would prefer to be talking to the people at their table rather than listening to the speaker, (3) most are at the event because they *had* to come, not because they *wanted* to come, and (4) most want to get the hell out at the earliest possible moment. If I anticipate interminable meanderings, I will sit as close to the door as possible to facilitate an early escape without detection.

The number of functions I *want* to attend, as against those I *have* to attend, are a precious few. For example, I always look forward to the Al Smith Dinner in October and the Friendly Sons of St. Patrick's Dinner on March 17. That's not merely because of their distinct Irish flavor, but primarily because of the extraordinary caliber of the speakers who address those august bodies and the enormous effort they put into their speeches. They know that at these dinners they are expected to excel, and most rise to the occasion. The late William Hughes Mulligan and the late Owen McGivern come readily to mind. Unfortunately, these special occasions are far outnumbered by the mind-numbing affairs you are pressured to attend for one reason or another.

It takes time and effort to be brief; you have to work at it. Winston Churchill once apologized to Franklin Roosevelt for sending him a long letter, explaining that he hadn't had the time to write a short one. On another occasion he intoned: "It is sheer laziness not compressing thought into a reasonable space."

Additionally you need not sacrifice your message for the sake of brevity. Lincoln's Gettysburg Address, one of the most powerful speeches ever delivered, contained 268 words and was over in less than three minutes!

This is a fitting place to point out the importance of delivering a "take away" message. You want your audience to remember the thrust of *what* you said, more than the *way* in which you said it. You want them talking about substance rather than style: your *speech* rather than *you*. Do not let that "take away" message drown in a sea of words.

So I urge you to be brief; if you are, you will be rewarded. The next time you attend an event and a speaker speaks briefly—take note of the applause that speaker receives. Having said so much about brevity, I better hurry on to the next chapter.

CHAPTER III

Stirring the Soul

In the main, public speaking has to do with stirring, exciting, touching and calming emotions. The words of the great orators illustrate the principle. Referring to Churchill's oratory during World War II, President John F. Kennedy, on the occasion of bestowing U.S. Citizenship on Churchill, said: "He mobilized the English language and sent it into battle." Indeed he did.

When the British Empire and the French Republic declared war against Nazi Germany, Churchill said:

> "We shall go on to the end, we shall fight in France, we shall fight on the seas and oceans, we shall fight with growing confidence and growing strength in the air, we shall defend our island, whatever the cost may be, we shall fight on the beaches, we shall fight on the landing grounds, we shall fight in the fields and in the streets, we shall fight in the hills; we shall never surrender."

Listen to his words when France surrendered in June 1940 (not an unusual happening): "Let us therefore brace ourselves to our duties, and so bear ourselves that, if the British Empire and its Commonwealth last for a thousand years, men will still say, 'This was their finest hour.'"

Later in 1940 he said: "Remember, we shall never stop, never weary, and never give in." And he underscored that resolve with: "The nose of the bulldog has been slanted backward so that he can breathe without letting go."

Finally, his tribute to the RAF pilots who fought so valiantly during the so called "Battle of Britain": "Never in the field of human conflict was so much owed by so many to so few."

President Franklin D. Roosevelt galvanized our nation for war with the speech he delivered on the day after the attack on Pearl Harbor:

> "Yesterday, December 7, 1941—a date which will live in infamy— the United States of America was suddenly and deliberately attacked by naval and air forces of the Empire of Japan . . . . No matter how long it may take us to overcome this premeditated invasion, the American people in their righteous might will win through to absolute victory . . . . Hostilities exist. There is no blinking at the fact that our people, our territory, and our interests are in grave danger. With confidence in our armed forces—with the unbounding determination of our people—we will gain the inevitable triumph—so help us God."

Douglas MacArthur touched the hearts of millions of Americans, including my own, when he addressed a joint session of Congress on April 19, 1951 after being relieved as the Supreme Commander of the United Nation Forces in Korea, by President Harry S. Truman:

> "The world has turned over many times since I took the oath on the plain at West Point, and the hopes and dreams have long since vanished, but I still remember the refrain of one of the most popular barracks ballads of that day which proclaimed most proudly that 'old soldiers never die; they just fade away.' And like the old soldier of that ballad, I now close my military career and just fade away,

an old soldier who tried to do his duty as God gave him the light
to see that duty. Good-bye."

There was no better speech writer than William Shakespeare, nor has anyone
ever decimated a person more effectively than the Bard's Mark Anthony, when
he heaped scorn and loathing on the shoulders of Brutus for his treacherous
murder of Julius Caesar. Listen to Shakespeare's description of Caesar and
the biting sarcasm he levels at Brutus:

> "But Brutus says he was ambitious;
> And Brutus is an honourable man.
> He had brought many captives home to Rome,
> Whose ransoms did the general coffers fill:
> Did this in Caesar seem ambitious?
> When that the poor have cried, Caesar hath wept:
> Ambition should be made sterner stuff:
> Yet Brutus says he was ambitious;
> And, sure, he is an honourable man.
> You all did see that on the Lupercal
> I thrice presented him a kingly crown,
> Which he did thrice refuse: was this ambition?
> Yet Brutus says he was ambitious;
> And, sure, he is an honourable man."

Some may be surprised that the technique of the *repetitive refrain* so deftly
employed by Shakespeare's Mark Anthony, has such a long history. Today's
politicians try to employ it regularly but usually without success. While it
can be an enormously powerful devise, it can also be catastrophic if not well
crafted and delivered. No one utilized that technique more brilliantly than
President John F. Kennedy when he addressed a crowd in front of the Berlin
Wall on June 26, 1963:

> "Two thousand years ago, the proudest boast was 'Civis Romanus
> sum!' (I am a citizen of Rome.) Today in the world of freedom, the
> proudest boast is 'Ich bin ein Berliner!' (I am a Berliner.)

There are many people in the world who really don't understand—or say they don't—what is the greatest issue between the free world and Communist world. *Let them come to Berlin!*

There are some who say that 'Communism is the wave of the future.' *Let them come to Berlin!*

And there are some who say in Europe and elsewhere, 'We can work with the Communists.' *Let them come to Berlin!*

And there are even a few who say 'Yes, that it's true, that communism is an evil system, but it permits us to make economic progress.' *Lass' sie nach Berlin en kommen! Let them come to Berlin!*

Freedom has many difficulties, and democracy is not perfect But we have never had to put a wall up to keep our people in, to prevent them from leaving us!"

No one, in my memory, ever received a more thunderous ovation!

There are two other oratorical features in Kennedy's speech worth noting. The use of Latin usually lends an erudite touch (whether or not deserved), and use of the native language of those in attendance, in this case German, is invariably well received providing, of course, it is pronounced and enunciated properly!

The repetitive refrain was again at work when Sojourner Truth addressed a Women's Convention in Akron, Ohio in 1851, on the subject of women's rights. No one ever touched *more* emotions than she, when she gave her "Ain't I A Woman" speech on that occasion. Here it is:

"Well, children, where this is so much racket there must be something out of kilter. I think that the negroes of the South and the women at the North, all talking about rights, the white men will be in a fix pretty soon. But what's all this here talking about?

That man over there says that women need to be helped into carriages, and lifted over ditches, and to have the best place everywhere. Nobody ever helps me into carriages, or over mud-puddles, or gives me any best place! And ain't I a woman? Look at me! Look at my arm! I have ploughed and planted, and gathered into barns, and no man could head me! And ain't I a woman? I could work as much and eat as much as a man—when I could get it—and bear the lash as well! And ain't I a woman? I have borne thirteen children, and seen most all sold off to slavery, and when I cried out with my mother's grief, none but Jesus heard me! And ain't I a woman?

Then they talk about this think in the head; what's this they call it? [member of audience whispers, "intellect"] That's it, honey. What's that got to do with women's rights or negroes' rights? If my cup won't hold but a pint, and yours hold a quart, wouldn't you be mean not to let me have my little half measure full?

Then that little man in black there, he says women can't have as much rights as men, 'cause Christ wasn't a woman!! Where did your Christ come from? Where did your Christ come from? From God and a woman! Man had nothing to do with Him.

If the first woman God ever made was strong enough to turn the world upside down all alone, these women together ought to be able to turn it back, and get it right side up again! And now they is asking to do it, the men better let them.

Obliged to you for hearing me, and now old Sojourner ain't got nothing more to say."

With those words, she makes you sad; she makes you laugh; she makes you angry; she lifts you up; she inspires you; she commands your respect and admiration; she chides you and finally she motivates you to carry out her will!

On March 4, 1865, as the Civil War was coming to a close, Abraham Lincoln sought to calm and bring together a deeply divided and terribly troubled nation in his second inaugural address. The final sentence, with its iambic pentameter, is sheer poetry:

> "With malice toward none; with charity for all; with firmness in the right, as God gives us to see the right, let us strive on to finish the work we are in; to bind up the nation's wounds; to care for him who shall have borne the battle, and for his widow, and his orphan—to do all which may achieve and cherish a just and a lasting peace, among ourselves and with all nations."

Sublime prose and poetry are frequently intertwined. Many literary elements more common to poetry can and should be employed in prose such as aliteration and onomatopoeia. Both of those elements were combined magnificently by Lord Byron in a line from *Don Juan*: "Wounded and fetter'd, cabin'd, cribb'd, confin'd"

But the speech which had more impact on our nation than any other during my life time, was the "I Have A Dream" speech which Martin Luther King, Jr. delivered on August 28, 1963. Fix King's anguished face in your minds eye and hear his words:

> "Let us not wallow in the valley of despair. I say to you today, my friends, that even though we face the difficulties of today and tomorrow. I still have a dream. It is a dream deeply rooted in the American dream.
>
> I have a dream that one day this nation will rise up and live out the true meaning of its creed. We hold these truths to be self-evident that all men are created equal.
>
> I have a dream that one day on the red hills of Georgia the sons of former slaves and the sons of former slave owners will be able to sit down together at the table of brotherhood.

I have a dream that one day even the state of Mississippi, a state sweltering with the heat of oppression, will be transformed into an oasis of freedom and justice.

I have a dream that my four little children will one day live in a nation where they will not be judged by the color of their skin but by the content of their character.

I have a dream today.

I have a dream that one day down in Alabama, with its vicious racists, with its governor having his lips dripping with the words of interposition and nullification; that one day right down in Alabama little black boys and black girls will be able to join hands with little white boys and white girls as sisters and brothers."

Once again the electrifying effect of the repetitive refrain.

The power of his final paragraph is stunning and will be felt by generations to come:

"And when this happens, when we let freedom ring, when we let it ring from every tenement and every hamlet, from every state and every city, we will be able to speed up that day when all of God's children, black men and white men, Jews and Gentiles, Protestants and Catholics, will be able to join hands and sing in the words of the old spiritual, 'Free at last, free at last. Thank God Almighty we are free at last.'"

After a magnificent career with the New York Yankees, Lou Gehrig was diagnosed with amyotrophic lateral sclerosis, a rare disease which causes spinal paralysis. On July 4, 1939 he stood before 60,000 fans at Yankee Stadium and said:

"Fans, for the past two weeks you have been reading about a bad break I got. Yet today I consider myself the luckiest man on the face of the earth."

He went on to thank and pay tribute to his fans, the Yankee organization, his fellow Yankees and his family. He ended with these words:

> "So I close in saying that I might have had a bad break—but I have an awful lot to live for."

Because of that speech, Lou Gehrig enjoys the adulation of our nation to this day.

Now it's not likely that you or I will be afforded an opportunity to speak in the kinds of circumstances I've described in this chapter, and obviously some situations lend themselves to stirring emotions more than others. But it's important that you do the best you can with what you have.

Here is one final note before leaving this topic. Many years ago, while on business at the Camelback Resort Hotel in Scottsdale, Arizona, I happened upon a large group of young salesmen employed by the Lay Potato Chip Company, all dressed alike in blue blazers, tan trousers, blue shirts and red ties. They were being addressed out-of-doors by an individual engaged in an all-out effort to motivate them. The speaker extolled all of the many virtues of the Lay potato chip as against all other kinds of potato chips and went on to suggest that the Lay potato chip was indeed one of America's great staples! He noted that Lay potato chips were reasonably priced and available to all Americans. There was even a veiled intimation that the selling of Lay Potato Chips was in the national interest, if not a patriotic imperative. I share this story with you to point out that while the stirring of emotions is important—some modicum of restraint is advisable!

Chapter IV

Humor

It is my opinion that humor is king in the realm of public speaking. Whether it is used to make a point or simply to make people laugh, it reigns supreme.

There are very important elements that are incorporated in the wonderful humor mixer that go beyond the spoken words. There is timing, delivery and persona; each varies with each individual.

One of the best examples of this mix is the humor of the late Jack Benny. I will never forget the episode in which a robber sticks a gun in Benny's back and says:

> *"Your money or your life."*

There followed a pause that seemed to go on forever, during which the audience became more and more hysterical. Finally, the robber repeats his threat:

> *"Your money or your life"*

to which Benny responds:

> *"I'm thinking, I'm thinking."*

The audience exploded; Benny then went into his famous "take" and another extended pause followed with the audience filling the room with cascades of rolling laughter.

If you simply read the spoken material, if you didn't see Benny do it, or if you didn't know him, especially his public image for being "cheap," you'd scratch your head and wonder what it was all about. The mere words on a sheet of paper would be meaningless.

Another great example of this is Ed Koch. Ed couldn't tell a joke if his life depended on it! He is fully aware of that and does not even try; yet, he's hysterical when he wants to be. It's *all* personality, facial expressions, shoulder shrugs, pauses, and yes "takes" which are distinctly "Koch."

My own humor is heavily dependent upon timing and delivery. I was keenly aware of that in 1985 when I wrote the speech that Senator Al D'Amato delivered before the Friendly Sons of St. Patrick. On the day of the speech, I spent the entire day with Al. I had him deliver that speech over and over and over again until he had it down to perfection.

All of that hard work paid off that night. Al, who had been scared to death, (particularly in the light of Senator Moynihan's earlier experience before the *not* so Friendly Sons), stood confidently before that very formidable audience in complete control and delivered his speech perfectly. His audience was laughing from beginning to end, and when he finished, he received a standing ovation in the "hall of the orators." Public speaking is a lot of hard work, but you have got to do it.

There are different forms of humor. Judge William Hughes Mulligan crafted hilarious apocryphal stories or made humorous observations and commentaries about events and circumstances, while Judge Owen McGivern preferred to slip "one liners." Both were magnificent.

There is "inside" humor such as you are apt to hear at a retirement dinner or a bachelor party.

There is humor that has a "bite" to it and requires a "target." However clever, that type of humor frequently causes an audience inner discomfort and, in my judgment, ranks below humor that does not offend. There is a difference between "kidding" someone and hurting someone's feelings. Audiences are repelled by the latter and often let a speaker know it! The master of "target" humor was Graucho Marx, but he was rarely hurtful. Don Rickles does it too, but he is often hurtful.

While creative humor is a God-given talent, there are approaches and mechanics that can assist. Humor is enhanced dramatically when it is *self effacing*. Audiences embrace it readily and enthusiastically because they relate to it. You can add a pinch of *tasteful irreverence* which invariably evokes laughter, but you have got to be careful.

"Dead panning" has to do with having a blank expression on your face. "Dead pan" when you deliver humorous lines and *continue* to "dead pan" after you've delivered them. It gives the humor an added lift. Most people don't appreciate speakers who laugh at their own material. I was present on countless occasions when Mulligan and McGivern delivered hilarious speeches, and I never saw either one of them crack a smile.

When your humor receives a favorable response, pause and don't go on until the laughter has run its course. Laughter begets laughter—and shouldn't be cut off. Incidentally, there is nothing more idiotic than a speaker chiding an audience for its failure to laugh at attempted humor that fails. And yet speakers, including professional comedians, do it all the time! There are ways to acknowledge that something hasn't gone over, but the way to do it is to blame yourself—*not* your audience!

Over the years I have heard a plethora of humorous stories and have used many of them time and again with success. The good ones never grow old. Obviously, they can't be plucked out of thin air but rather have to fit, however loosely, with what is happening.

In 1996 we opened Wagner Park at Hugh L. Carey Battery Park City. As Chairman of Battery Park City Authority, it was my job to introduce the speakers for the occasion: Mayor Rudy Guiliani, Governor George E. Pataki and former Mayor Ed Koch. When I introduced Guiliani I referred to him as "the battling, two fisted Mayor of the City of New York". When Rudy commenced his remarks, he noted that my introduction was more in the vein of introducing a prize fighter than a public official. When I returned to the microphone I made reference to Rudy's comment and went on to tell the story of "Nonetheless." It's my favorite story and it goes like this:

> Years ago when Madison Square Garden was located at 8th Avenue and 50th Street, we had boxing matches on Friday nights. On one such occasion, Johnny Addy, the ring announcer, entered the ring to announce the main event. He banged on the bell to get attention and a hush came over the garden. He then said: "Gladys Gooding will now sing and play the national anthem." At that point a drunk in the balcony got up and hollered at the top of his lungs: "Gladys Gooding is a no good Goddamn whore"—to which Addy responded:—"*Nonetheless*" . . . .

This is a picture of me delivering the punch line. I violated one of my own basic rules by failing to "dead pan." I just couldn't help myself! In the background from left to right are: Governor George Pataki, Mayor Rudy Giuliani and former Mayor Ed Koch.

The following are other stories I've told over the years and I invite you to use any of them if they suit a situation. I can assure you that they are not my exclusive property, as many will attest.

Cardinal Cushing

Many years ago there was a terrible fire at Filenes Department Store in Boston and Father Richard Cushing, later to become Richard Cardinal Cushing, the Archbishop of Boston, responded. Upon his arrival, he saw a man lying on the ground *in extremis*. Father Cushing knelt down next to the man to give him the Last Rights. He then bent over him and whispered in his ear "Do you believe in God the Father, God the Son, and God the Holy Ghost" whereupon the man on the ground opened one eye and responded: *"I'm dying—and you want me to answer a riddle?"*

About the Irish

William Hughes Mulligan loved to tell the story of the Irishman who, when asked that most welcome question, "Will you have another drink?" responded: "I've only answered that question in the negative once—*and that time I didn't understand the question.*"

• • •

An Irish couple celebrated their 50th Wedding Anniversary by attending a Cana Conference. On their way home, the husband turned to his wife and said: "Kate, did we ever have conjugal relations?" "I don't know" answered Kate,—*"but if we did, they didn't come to your father's wake."*

• • •

Two Irishman were on the way to the Parish House to take the pledge when one said "Let's have one more drink before we take the pledge." "No" responded the other, "he'll smell it on our breathe—*we'll have it when we come out.*"

• • •

Ireland entered a figure skater in the Olympic Games. No sooner did he get out on the ice when he fell down—and then fell down again and again. The German judge and the French judge both gave him a zero while the Irish judge gave him a perfect score. The head of the games castigated the Irish judge: "You've disgraced yourself, Ireland and the Olympic games by your blatant and outrageous partisanship". "There was no partisanship at all" responded the Irish judge—*"it was very slippery out there."*

• • •

This is the transcript of a radio conversation between a British ship and the Irish off the coast of Kerry which took place in October 1995. The radio transcript was released by the British Chief of Naval Operations on October 10, 1995.

"IRISH: Please divert your course 15 degrees to the *South* to avoid a collision.

BRITISH: Recommend you divert your course 15 degrees to the *North* to avoid a collision.

IRISH: Negative—you will have to divert your course 15 degrees to the *South* to avoid a collision.

BRITISH: This is the Captain of a British naval vessel—I say again, divert *your* course.

IRISH: Negative—I say again—You will have to divert *your* course.

BRITISH: THIS IS THE AIRCRAFT CARRIER HMS BRITANNIA—THE SECOND LARGEST SHIP IN THE BRITISH ATLANTIC FLEET.—WE ARE ACCOMPANIED BY THREE DESTROYERS, THREE CRUISERS AND NUMEROUS SUPPORT VESSELS. I DEMAND THAT YOU CHANGE YOUR COURSE 15 DEGREES NORTH. I SAY AGAIN—THAT IS 15 DEGREES NORTH—OR COUNTER MEASURES WILL BE UNDERTAKEN TO ENSURE THE SAFETY OF THIS SHIP.

IRISH: *WE ARE A LIGHTHOUSE. YOUR CALL.*"

My dear friend B.J. Harrington gave me that one years ago and I've been using it ever since, *without* attribution of course! By the way, Harrington never told me where *he* got it either!

Churchill's Wit

Churchill had it all, including humor.[1] People sometimes question whether some of the Churchill stories are true or whether they are properly attributed to him. The answer is that the stories are wonderful and who cares. In addition, they can be incorporated into speeches easily and in a host of ways.

Here's a taste: Lady Astor once said to Churchill: "Mr. Prime Minster, if I were married to you I would put poison in your coffee." To which he responded: *"Madam if I were married to you, I would drink it!"*

● ● ●

On another occasion Lady Astor said to Churchill: "Mr. Prime Minister I'm told that if we were to pour all of the whiskey you've drunk during your

---

[1] "The Wit and Wisdom of Winston Churchill" by James C. Humes, is a treasure trove of Churchillian humor.

lifetime into this room, it would be half full." *"Ah yes" replied Churchill, "So much has been accomplished—but there's so much more to do."*

• • •

Churchill was attending a cocktail party in Quebec and in the presence of a stodgy Methodist Archbishop when a waitress offered them glasses of wine. The Archbishop chided the waitress saying: "Young lady I would sooner commit adultery before allowing alcohol to pass my lips." As the waitress moved away, Churchill, who had accepted one of the glasses, hollered after her: *"Come back here lass—I didn't know we had a choice!"*

• • •

There is a famous picture of Charles de Gaulle with a shocked expression on his face. Churchill undoubtedly had that picture in mind when he said: *"Charles de Gaulle looks like a female llama, suddenly startled in the midst of her bath!"*

• • •

In 1931 George Bernard Shaw wired Churchill as follows: "Am reserving two tickets for you on opening night for my new play. Come and bring a friend—if you have one." Churchill's response: "Impossible for me to attend first performance. Would like to attend second night—*if there is one.*"

Which incidentally brings to mind an exchange between George Bernard Shaw and a beautiful young actress. "Mr. Shaw," she said "I want you to father my child. Can you imagine a child with my looks and your brains?" To which Shaw answered: "A tempting proposition indeed but I'm troubled by the notion of a child—*with my looks and your brains.*"

Some Jewish Stories

New York City has had a large Jewish population for many decades. Like so many religious, racial and ethnic groups that have come to the "melting pot," it has permeated our culture. Jewish humor is unique and precious—it is also universal. You don't have to be Jewish to enjoy Jewish humor. Here are some examples:

An Orthodox Jewish couple went to the Rabbi to discuss their wedding plans. "May we have a celebration in connection with our wedding?" asked the prospective groom. "Of course" said the Rabbi. "May we serve wine at the celebration?" "Of course" said the Rabbi. "May we have dancing at the celebration?" "No good" said the Rabbi—"too close—too much touching—too dangerous." "Well Rabbi, *after* we get married may we have sex?" the prospective groom inquired. "Oh yes" said the Rabbi "It's important to perpetuate the race." "Well Rabbi, after we get married may we have 'kinky' sex?" "So what's 'kinky' sex?" asked the Rabbi. "Rabbi, it would be like having sex while standing up."—"No good" thundered the Rabbi—*"it could lead to dancing."*

• • •

The following is a silly story but I love it. A man went into Ratners Delicatessen and ordered a herring. When the herring came the man picked up his knife and was about to cut into the herring when the herring said: "Please don't hurt me."

The man ran out of Ratners in a panic and despite his great love for herring, didn't return for six months. Finally he got up enough courage to return and he ordered another herring. As soon as the herring came, he picked up his knife and herring said: "Please don't kill me"—and the man ran out of Ratners again.

Two years later the man was in Miami, Florida salivating for a herring. Finally he slipped into Wolfies Delicatessen, took a seat in the back booth, motioned to the waiter and quietly ordered a herring. When the herring came he picked up his knife whereupon the herring looked up and said:

"What's the matter—you don't like Ratners no more?"

• • •

This is a *true* story. Saul Pearce, who was one of the founding partners of our law firm and a delightful soul, used to take his mother to the Yiddish theatre every Sunday afternoon.

On one such occasion the show was about a young man who loaned his wife's father $1,000 on the young man's wedding day. A year later the young man sheepishly asked the father-in-law to repay the $1,000. The father-in-law said to the young man: "Do you have anything in writing to prove that you loaned me the $1,000?"—"No" replied the young man. "Well do you have any witnesses who saw you loan me the $1,000." "No" answered the anguished young man, whereupon Saul's mother got up in the audience and shouted:

"I saw it!"

Ad Libbing

Ad libbing is also an art and not for the faint of heart or inexperienced. When done properly however, it's dynamite.

The late John Cardinal O'Connor was one of the fastest guns in town when it came to ad libbing. At a luncheon at the Grand Hyatt to raise money for the Inner-City Archdiocesan Schools, I mistakenly introduced him as "*John Cardinal Spellman.*" It just slipped out! When the laughter subsided I said: "I think I just lost a client." When the Cardinal took the rostrum he opened with: "James, you didn't just *lose* a client, you *buried* me!"

In 2003 we opened the "Solaire" at Battery Park City, the first high rise residential "green" building in the world, and I was on the program. Prior speakers described in great depth and in excruciating scientific detail the many environmental features of the building and went on at considerable length to catalogue its many medical advantages. When it finally came my turn to speak, I said: "On the basis of what we've heard this morning, it's my understanding that this building is so advanced medically—that if a person were to move in and never come out—*that person would live to be at least 150 years old!*

This is a picture of me delivering that line. This time I *did* "dead pan." Governor George Pataki is standing behind me at the far right of the picture.

By the way, some have been known to *prepare* "ad libs" in advance—not I! And many people who are called upon to make public pronouncements regularly, such as politicians, have canned modules on a variety of subjects etched into their brains which "pop out" whenever one of those subjects arises. A good audience will detect a pre-fabricated "ad lib."

PART 2

Types of Speeches

For the remainder of this book, we will look at some of the various kinds of speeches we are called upon to deliver, i.e., the introduction, the eulogy, the "after dinner" speech, the "roast", etc. Although the various kinds of speeches have special features, all of the general principles we have discussed are always in play, especially brevity and levity.

Chapter V

Political Speeches

(Honesty + Sincerity = Credibility)

No discussion of public speaking can ignore the type of speech to which we are subjected most frequently: the political speech. Speeches delivered by political candidates to solicit votes, in the main, are the worst. For that kind of speech to work, the speaker must project honesty and sincerity. Strangely enough, the best way to accomplish that is to be honest and sincere!

Honesty

Politicians who willfully and deliberately tell untruths to the American people to protect or promote themselves politically, lose credibility immediately and rarely get it back. The American people are a tolerant and forgiving people—but history tells us that they will neither tolerate nor forgive lying; nor should they. Truth-telling is one of the most important cornerstones of an ordered society. It is axiomatic that if a person will lie about one thing, that person is likely to lie about another; either you respect the truth or you don't. Finally, so called "spinning", which has come into vogue over the last decade, is nothing more than playing "fast and loose" with the truth.

There are some misguided souls who say that politicians running for office should be granted leeway with respect to telling the truth; that "toying" with the truth or "fudging" is part of the "political game." *I could not disagree more*. Indeed, those seeking political office should be held to an even *higher* standard than others because of the enormous impact they have on society. A mayor, a governor, a president, a legislator or a judge can affect more lives with the sweep of a pen than most people in the private sector affect in a lifetime. Many politicians and their advisors underestimate the ability of the American people to detect "slipping and sliding." It is easy for the average person to spot a phony, and it is a terrible miscalculation for anyone seeking the public trust.

When politicians make mistakes, they should admit them in the most straightforward way possible. While Americans will not accept lying in any form or under any pseudonym, they are most understanding, forgiving and even kindly disposed towards those who say: "I'm sorry, I made a mistake and I will do my best to insure that it doesn't happen again." That's because Americans know that we are all human and we all make mistakes.

Some politicians and others as well, have great difficulty admitting a mistake or offering an apology; some even try to cover up. Amazingly enough, to this day, there are *still* those who do not realize that a "cover up" is infinitely more stupid and dangerous than the underlying transgression.

There are also those who try to apologize without apologizing. It goes like this: "*If* I've offended any one by what I've said . . ." That's not an apology—it's a reaffirmation of what the offending party said originally and a suggestion that the complaining party had no basis for taking offense! Such an "apology" does not put the problem to rest. Jesse Jackson's apology for referring to New York as "Hymie Town" and Prince Harry's apology for wearing a Nazi uniform, are examples.

Al D'Amato is my dear friend. While still a member of the U.S. Senate and during the trial of O.J. Simpson, Al went on "Imus in the Morning" and imitated Judge Ito, who is a Japanese American.

I happened to be in Al's office in Washington, D.C. when all hell broke loose. He showed me a draft of an apology which had been prepared for him and he asked for my thoughts. The apology was one of those "*If* I've offended anyone" non-apologies and was quickly jettisoned. I stayed with Al for the rest of that day and the next. During that time, he called every Japanese American in the Senate and in the House and personally tendered an unconditional, abject apology. When he spoke with his dear friend U.S. Senator Danny Inouye of Hawaii, a great American hero who lost an arm during World War II, he broke down and cried. His crying was so intense and deeply felt, I almost cried myself.

Al then went on the Senate floor and offered the same kind of apology to Judge Ito. During the apology he castigated himself, especially in view of the discrimination which had been visited upon Italians for decades. The next morning he went on "Good Morning America" and repeated the apology. Al was genuinely ashamed of himself; he did the right thing, in the right way and a very unfortunate occurrence was over, once and for all. Incidentally, Senator Inouye could not have been more gracious.

All of this is by way of saying that mistakes should be dealt with forthrightly and openly. Not only is it the right thing to do, but it will enhance credibility. Similarly, if an opponent does or says something you believe is right—say so! President Kennedy was wont to say: "If you do what's right, usually it will be right politically."

Tom Foley, the Democratic leader who launched the magnificent career of Al Smith, gave him a piece of political advice when he was first elected to the New York State Assembly, which Smith valued and followed consistently throughout his career. Foley told him: "Don't ever make a promise you can't keep." That also goes to *honesty*.

Sincerity

Sincerity is related to honesty, but goes beyond it. It has more to do with the ability to convey that you truly believe in what you are saying because it is right. This is the aspect of public speaking where God-given natural talent counts the most, although there are ideological under-pinnings which can assist.

A person in the political arena must develop an over-all governmental philosophy and embrace it with conviction. That does not mean that *all* issues must fit neatly within that over-all frame work, particularly since the number of political issues has burgeoned. To the contrary, each issue should be considered individually *on the merits,* and if positions result that do not square perfectly with over-arching political philosophy, so be it. More than that, if you find that *all* issues are in *full* accord with over-all rubric, you run the risk of being considered a non-thinking ideologue, and understandably so; that flies in the face of human nature and experience.

Former Mayor Ed Koch, when running for office, used to say "If you agree with me on 8 issues out of 12, vote for me. If you agree with me on all 12 issues, see a psychiatrist." The notion of "I'm a this or I'm a that and so on this issue I've got to be here or there" has worked for some in the past, but it is yesterday. Americans are becoming less and less interested in labels and blind loyalty to political causes or parties and more and more supportive of politicians who act from conscience—even if they disagree with their conclusions. The day of the political automaton is coming to a close, and the day of the political hybrid is in ascendancy. Moreover, vote-casting on the basis of race, religion or ethnicity is fading.

You need a plan and you have got to be *consistent*. You can't change positions on the basis of polls or shifting political winds. That tells your listeners that you do not act from conviction but rather that you will say whatever is necessary to garner votes. That is *deadly*. You can change your mind if there is a reasonable basis for doing so—but not every month!

You have got to say the same thing, no matter where you are or to whom you say it. You could get away with taking varying positions before different groups of people years ago, but this is the age of instant and total communication. It is also important to avoid pandering to interest groups. It's perfectly all right to support the programs of interest groups, but do it on the merits so that you can make the case convincingly when called upon to do so.

Perhaps the best way to convey sincerity is to take a position which you truly believe in, despite the fact that it is unpopular. The positions taken by those portrayed in *Profiles in Courage* a book written by a very young John F. Kennedy are examples. "Courage," that's the word, and that's the quality that Americans admire most.

Negative Attacks

Of course you have to confront and take issue with a political opponent. You would be well advised however, to do so on a high plane and in a dignified manner. I am appalled by the lack of common civility on the part of some of today's politicians, and so are most Americans. Not that all politicians of the past were models of civility. Take the battle between Alexander Hamilton and Aaron Burr for instance; that classic rivalry underscores the high price one can pay for indulging in *ad hominem* language.

Words such as "liar", "ignorant", "incompetent", "arrogant" and "pompous" are highly offensive and repel everyone except of course "frothing at the mouth" political fanatics and haters at both ends of the political spectrum whose votes are already irrevocably committed. Those kinds of vicious personal attacks gain you *nothing* and cost you appreciably.

But if you *must* do it, do it with panache and humor, which brings us back once again to Winston Churchill. Listen to the manner in which he attacked his political adversaries.

Of Stanley Baldwin he said: "Occasionally he stumbled over the truth but hastily picked himself up as if nothing had happened."

Of Clement Attlee he said: "He is a modest man with much to be modest about."

Of Sir Stafford Cripps he said: "There but for the grace of God goes God."

But it is always a special joy when one politician gives another his or her come-uppance for engaging in an *ad hominem* attack. Governor Al Smith was born in a tenement house on Oliver Street on the lower East side of New York—a far cry from being "born to the purple." He had been the three term Governor of New York and during the course of his fourth gubernatorial campaign, was viciously attacked again and again for "conducting himself like a king." At the end of one such attack, Smith thrust his arms in the air and shouted: "Behold the King—the King from Oliver Street!"

Incidentally, Franklin D. Roosevelt delivered one of the greatest political speeches ever uttered when he placed Al Smith in nomination for president at the Democratic Convention in 1924. He concluded his nominating speech with a ringing quotation from William-Wordsworth:

"This is the Happy Warrior; this is he

Whom every man in arms should wish to be."

From that moment forward Al Smith was known as "The Happy Warrior."

CHAPTER VI

Introductions and Eulogies

Introductions

Introducing an honoree or a principal speaker is a common form of public speaking. In preparing your introduction, bear in mind that the speech should be about the *honoree* and not about *you*—a very basic concept frequently disregarded. Also, take the time to learn the things of which the *honoree* is most proud. A little license is permissible, for the sake of humor!.

On September 21, 1990, I introduced Judge William Hughes Mulligan at a luncheon to raise funds for the Inner-City Archdiocesan schools. It was attended by 500 lawyers and judges at the Grand Hyatt Hotel in New York. During the luncheon, His Eminence John Cardinal O'Connor, presented Judge Mulligan with the St. Thomas More Award.

I began my remarks as follows:

> "It was clear from the outset that Judge Mulligan would be a brilliant legal scholar. At the age of two months he uttered his first words which were: 'Res Ipsa loquitur'. Two weeks later he scrawled the words: 'Quare clausum fregit' on the floor in his playpen."

For non-Lawyers, "*Res upsa loquitur*" is legal principle meaning "The thing speaks for itself" and "*Quare clausum fregit*" is an old English legal writ.

I then repeated the most humorous excerpts I could find from Mulligan's previous speeches, much to the delight of the audience. More importantly, *he* was enormously pleased. There was no need to tell the audience who Mulligan was or what he had done—everyone in the room knew that.

Eulogies

I have given many eulogies for friends and relatives and I don't like doing it because it is an enormous emotional drain. I always steel myself in advance to get over what I anticipate will be the "rough spots", but you never know what's going to come up and hit you out of the blue. It's rough, but it's impossible to say "No" when you're asked to do one—at least I can't.

The most important aspect of doing a eulogy is to capture the *essence* of the person you are eulogizing. A eulogy does not have to be a dirge. To the contrary, some tasteful humor can lighten the pain and provide some respite.

I have been around a long time and I have met a lot of people, but the most fascinating person I ever met was Jack Reilly. He was born on the Lower East side of New York and he rarely left it. Jack was an active Republican in an area that was very heavily Democratic and spent a life time in the boxing business as a trainer, a manager and an owner.

He was the savviest person I ever met. He had a sense of humor that was unique and the best I've ever witnessed. There was not an ounce of baloney in Jack and everyone who knew him loved him.

Here's a picture of Jack with the heavy weight champion of the world, Joe Louis, when they were in the Army together during World War II. Louis is on the far right and Jack is standing next to him at the microphone.

Jack and I were close friends, and when Jack died, his wife Helen and his sons, Johnny and Paul asked me to deliver the eulogy at his funeral mass at Immaculate Conception Church on 14th Street and First Avenue.

Jack had more moving parts than anyone I ever knew, but I poured my heart and soul into the effort and I think I caught the essence of Jack Reilly. As you read it, try to pick out some of the principles we've been discussing, such as humor, the repetitive refrain, tasteful irreverence, stirring emotions, the "take away" message, and brevity. You will also find a reference to *Jack's* "dead panning." Here's some of what I said:

> "I first met Jack in the early 50's when we were both students
> at Fordham Law School. From the very beginning, there was

an intriguing aura about Jack. He had been in the Army during World War II and had served in the European Theatre. When he got out of the Army, he went into the boxing business as a trainer, a manager and an owner.

Over the years he had had a host of fighters including 'Popeye' Woods and one of the finest boxers in the game 'Irish' Billy Graham. Jack had graduated from Fordham undergraduate school—and had applied to attend Fordham Law School on a bet.—When he was accepted, he collected the bet and decided to attend.

But when school began, Jack had to go to Havana, Cuba, where his fighter, 'Irish' Billy Graham was fighting 'Kid' Gavilan for the welterweight championship of the world. The fight was nationally televised and Gavilan won a highly controversial split decision over Graham.

By the time Jack returned from Havana—he had missed the first month of school. When he finally showed up for class—he was ordered to report immediately to the office of the very austere Dean Ignatius M. Wilkinson.

When Jack explained to the Dean where he had been—Wilkinson's eyes lit up—and for the next hour and a half, Jack and the Dean were sparring around the Dean's office—with the Dean lecturing Jack on what Graham had done wrong in the Gavilan fight.—While Jack didn't think a great deal of Wilkinson's boxing knowledge—the two of them got along swimmingly thereafter—and Jack never had any more trouble.

Everyone knew that Jack was considerably older than the rest of us—but no one knew *how much* older—and Jack wasn't telling. As a matter of fact, we still don't know how old Jack was.

Another cause for speculation was his ethnicity. The consensus was that he was part Native American but no one really knew—and Jack wasn't telling. However, as the rest of us got older looking, Jack continued to look just as he did the first day I saw him.

Jack literally created his own language. He had an entire lexicon of words, phrases and expressions and it took a while before you understood what he was talking about. But once you did, it was sheer delight simply because Jack had the greatest sense of humor in the world. I once said to him: 'Jack, Damon Runyon had nothing on you.' to which he responded: 'He traveled in limited circles.'—And with all of the magnificent humor he generated he never laughed himself. He was *always* the great stone face.

He was a quintessential New Yorker and never left the East Side, except when it was absolutely necessary. He knew this town and everybody in it—and everyone knew Jack. He had more street smarts than anyone I've ever met. But most of all, he knew people and could smell a phony a block away. No one, but no one, could fool Jack Reilly. He was straight up and never took himself seriously. He had no airs and no hidden agenda. No one awed him and he spoke his mind plainly and simply. When someone did or said something that Jack didn't like, that person would be declared 'Out of order'.

He was actively engaged in Republican politics and became the close friend of Vince Albano, the powerful Republican leader whom Jack dubbed 'Vince the Prince'—and it stuck.

Jack had a nickname for everyone. There was 'Jake the Snake'; 'Louie the Fish'; 'Chicken Pot Pie:' 'The Hat'; 'The Gum-Shoe'; 'The Cheerleader'; 'The Monkey'; 'The Horse'; 'The Saint'; 'The Chimp'; 'The Brain:' 'The Boyscout'; 'The Beast'—and a few others that I can't mention in this setting.

Jack paid his highest compliment to a person when he referred to that person as being 'legitimate'—or as being a 'citizen'.—

Later Jack served as general counsel to the Hotel Workers Union—until Governor Rockefeller appointed him as the Deputy Commissioner of Labor in charge of unemployment. I was with Jack shortly after his appointment and I said: 'How's the new job going?' Jack said: 'It's ok, except that every morning when I go to work—they think I'm one of the applicants!'—That was Jack.

Shortly thereafter, Jack became an adjunct professor of labor law at Delaware Law School and I frequently acted as a guest lecturer for him on Saturdays. Every time we got off the train in Wilmington, the same student who was in Jack's class would drive us to the Law School and then drive us back to the train when class ended. I finally said to Jack: 'What is it with that kid?' and Jack answered 'He gets an A + that's our deal'.—that was Jack.

Jack loved our law school and was enormously proud of the fact that he was a Fordham Law School graduate. A year and a half ago, and after he had become ill, Jack was honored by our law school for distinguished service as a judge. The plaque that I gave Jack on that occasion was displayed in his casket throughout his wake and went to his grave. Jack's sons Johnny and Paul told me that that's the way Jack wanted it.

Last fall I had lunch with Jack at a nearby restaurant. He, of course, knew he was dying and it didn't phase him a bit. He was hilarious as always. 'Helen is driving me crazy' he said. 'Every time I turn around she's got a priest in the apartment sprinkling me with holy water.—If she keeps it up, I won't die of cancer—I'll drown!'

Jack wasn't afraid to die because he had no reason to be afraid of death. Even with all of his bombastic talk he did not have a mean bone in his body nor did he ever intentionally inflict pain on another human being. He did a great deal with his life, but most of all, he brought joy, happiness and laughter into the lives of others.

And now we're all experiencing enormous pain because we feel we've lost Jack.—I certainly am—and have been since I learned of his death from his sons last Monday—

But we know that love places the well being of the person loved above one's own well being. And while it's true that we're all suffering—Jack is just fine. As a matter of fact, he has never been better. I am sure that by now Jack has nicknames for everyone in Heaven. I can hear him now, referring to God the Father as 'The Old Man'; to Jesus as 'The Kid'—and the Holy Spirit as 'The Spook'.

We would all do well to emulate Jack Reilly—because he was the best."

CHAPTER VII

Acceptances and Dedications

Acceptances

The recipient of an award should not merely express gratitude but make remarks that are in some way related to the award itself.

In 1993 I received the Charles Carroll of Carrollton Award from the Catholic Lawyers Guild at the Union League Club and was named "Catholic Lawyer of the Year."

During the ceremony I said:

> "When I was told that I was to be the recipient of the Charles Carroll of Carrollton Award—I decided to study the life of Charles Carroll of Carrollton—for the purpose of determining whether there were sufficient similarities between his life and mine—to warrant the granting of this Award to me.—After exhaustive research I am constrained to report that the answer is no.—While there are some similarities—they are overwhelmingly outweighed by the dissimilarities.
>
> Charles Carroll was born in colonial Annapolis which was described by one author as the 'most genteel place in North America.' I was

born in Waterbury, Connecticut, a factory town in the Naugatuck Valley—which in a recent poll was determined to be—'the least desirable city in the United States—in which to live.'

While Carroll was Irish—as am I—Carroll was descended from Irish Kings—whereas my ancestors, as best I can determine—were, in the main—gun-runners, rum runners, drunkards and horse thieves.

Of the Carroll family its been written 'Few American families had a more indisputable background of aristocracy in the Old World or could be more accurately described as aristocratic in the New.'—Of the Gills its been said—'They're of dubious origin—and can't be trusted under any set of circumstances.—They're devious, shifty-eyed—and harpies on the vitals of the poor!'

And, of course, Charles Carroll was one of the signers of the Declaration of Independence—and the only Catholic signor.—While I am also a Catholic—I did *not* sign the Declaration of Independence—although I would have—if given the opportunity.

Charles Carroll's cousin—John Carroll was the first Bishop in America. My most successful relative is a bookie in Philadelphia.

And when Carroll died, he was universally acknowledged as the wealthiest man in the United States—whereas I'm currently struggling to get enough cash—to get my shirts out of the cleaners!!!

To tell you the truth, the more I read about Charles Carroll of Carrollton—the more he got on my nerves.—And by the time I finished, I couldn't stand the guy.

Nonetheless, I never saw an award I didn't like—and I accept this one in his name with pride and gratitude—and before you decide to withdraw it!

I warn you, however, that henceforth I expect to be referred to as 'James Gill of Waterbury.'"

As I'm sure you're aware, the foregoing features the self-effacing humor and the irreverence we discussed earlier.

Dedications

Dedications, by their nature, are serious and solemn events. The most important aspect of a dedication is that you go to the heart of the dedication.

On July 16, 2002 we dedicated the Irish Hunger Memorial at Battery Park City. Here is part of what I said:

"The aspect of this Memorial that I savor the most is that it is truly a *living* Memorial. The landscaping is authentically Irish and will remain so. More than 60 species of Irish plants and grasses have taken root in this Memorial. It will be meticulously maintained and without the use of chemicals!

There are stones throughout the Memorial from every County in Ireland, North and South, symbolizing a united Ireland of 32 counties.

The texts on the sides and in the interior of the Memorial setting forth quotes, newspapers reports, poetry and literature about The Hunger, are changeable and will be replaced regularly.

Soon, there will be a World Hunger Library housed next to the Memorial containing books, writings and reports concerning The Hunger.

Finally, and most importantly, the Memorial will be equipped with audio messages that will bring attention to starvation wherever or whenever it occurs through the world. In conjunction with the United Nations, we will work to assist in the distribution of food to those areas.

Ladies and gentlemen, the wonderful Memorial before us today is not just another 'man on a horse.' It is a very special achievement, and needless to say we are enormously proud of it."

In 1997 we dedicated the New York Police Department Memorial at Battery Park City which bears the names of every Police Officer killed in the line of duty. In 2002 we added the names of the police officers killed on 9/11/01. My comments included the following:

"The most basic and fundamental—by far the strongest instinct in human kind—is the instinct for self-preservation. It prevails over all else—almost always. Those we honor today, overcame that primordial instinct and gave their lives to save the lives of others. In the doing, they left behind treasured loved ones. Would you do what they did—would I?

Only those who have been touched by a special spirit of duty and honor; only those possessed of the most powerful commitment, have it within them to make that kind of supreme sacrifice. There is no higher calling, there is no more noble virtue."

Chapter VIII

After Dinner Speeches and "Roasts"

After Dinner Speeches

The after dinner speech is sometimes a challenge. Frequently it is difficult to get and hold the attention of the audience because it is otherwise engaged, a bit intoxicated, and somewhat slowed by a heavy meal. The first rule is not to start until the audience settles down. The second rule is to start with something that will capture attention; if you capture audience attention *early*, the chances of keeping it are enhanced dramatically. An example of an "attention grabber": I was the speaker at the Friendly Sons of St. Patrick's dinner in 1992 and started by making reference to a *very embarrassing moment* in the life of St. Patrick when he officiated at the Baptismal ceremony of one of Ireland's first kings.

> "As we all know, St. Patrick had a spike at the end of his pastoral staff, to help him negotiate Ireland's rough terrain. At the very outset of the ceremony, he inadvertently stuck his staff into the King's foot. After the service had gone on for about fifteen minutes, Patrick looked down and observed that the King's foot was in a pool of blood! He immediately withdrew the staff, apologized and said 'Your Highness why didn't you say something' to which the King responded: *'I thought it was part of the ceremony'.*"

I will digress for a moment, to talk briefly about another technique which is sometimes referred as the "look back". It has to do with a second reference to some subject matter which was previously well received. The line in my opening. ("*I thought it was part of the ceremony*") evoked laughter, as I thought it would. My closing words were:

> "May the great Saint Patrick bless everyone in this room, particularly my own sons Patrick and Dennis. And gentlemen, when you get to heaven and meet Saint Patrick personally, *beware of his pastoral staff.* Thank you and Erin Go Bragh."

One final note, the serious portion of an after dinner speech should be reserved until the end.

The Roast

The key to the roast is to distill the target's known foibles and weaknesses and blow them out of proportion—*without being hurtful.*

Every year, the Association of the Bar of the City of New York conducts a "roast" of a public figure called the "Twelfth Night" which begins with a play performed by lawyers wherein the target is disparaged. The target's "defender" then refutes the charges but is really expected to lampoon the target further. In 1990 I was Ed Koch's "defender" and the following was part of my defense:

> "Many of the charges leveled against Ed are grossly exaggerated and enormously overblown. Take for instance the allegation that Ed has been intemperate and overly self-indulgent in his attacks upon persons with whom he disagrees or whom he dislikes.
>
> Now, I know that Ed referred to Leona Helmsley as the 'Wicked Witch of the West' and the 'Queen of Mean'.

And there's no denying the fact that he called Jimmy Breslin a 'bumble brain and a jerk'.

And I will admit that he labeled Ruth Messinger an 'ideologue and a bomb-thrower'.

And, yes, he referred to Arafat as an 'international hoodlum';

And we all know that he called Jay Goldin a 'snake in the grass.'

And I'm aware that he called Carole Bellamy a 'dingbat';

Jerry Ford an 'empty suit'.

And yes, it's widely known that he called Jesse Jackson an 'anti-Semite'; and Imelda Marcos a 'crook';

And no one need remind me that he called Kurt Waldheim a 'Nazi pig'; and

Ronald Lauder a 'clown'.

And I don't need to be told that the called Al Sharpton a 'racist';

Gary Hart a 'turkey' and

Donald Trump a 'hot dog'.

And, obviously, I will concede that he called Jack Newfield a 'hump'.

Dan Quayle a 'numb nut' and

Nancy Reagan a 'Barbie doll'.

But that's about it!

I mean—What's the big deal here?

Moreover, I would point out that during all of his years in public office, Ed never said a single unkind word about Mother Theresa, despite the fact that *she was constantly on his nerves.*

Another scurrilous charge leveled against Ed is that after becoming Mayor of New York, he sold out his liberal principles and became an arch conservative. For example, they point to the fact that shortly after Ed became Mayor, he called for the return of public flogging.

And of course, many make reference to the fact that Ed not only favors the death penalty, but a return of the firing squad.

And they make great to-do over Ed's recommendation that wolves be permitted to roam the MTA train yards as an anti-graffiti measure.

And, yes, they've pounced upon Ed's advocacy of the simultaneous invasions of Cuba, Nicaragua and the Canadian Province of Quebec.

And more recently, they've alluded to Ed's position that Noriega be tortured and hung in public without benefit of a trial.

On the basis of these perfectly reasonable, middle of the road proposals, Ed's enemies have labeled him a conservative!"

Chapter IX

Conclusion

As I have suggested, great orators and exceptional public speakers are born, not made. When they write their speeches, they instinctively incorporate the elements and techniques we have discussed and their timing and delivery flow naturally. But persons of intelligence and reasonable speaking ability can do very well if they apply the principles and ideas about which we've talked and if they are willing to work hard. A sense of humor also helps.

Public speaking is becoming more and more important as we move through a world of ever increasing communication. In many areas, it has become essential to success. I hope this book helps you and I wish you well.

As I said: "Brevity is a virtue."

The End

ACKNOWLEDGEMENT

I am deeply grateful to my dear friend Patrick F.X. Mulhearn, Bernadette Mulhearn, and my son, Patrick for all of their help in producing this book.